God's Pinky Promises

Written by Dawn Hood
Illustrations by Ron Wheeler

Published by
Inknbeans Press

©2012

© August 2012 Dawn Hood
and Inknbeans Press

Cover and interior illustrations conceived by
Dawn Hood
and created by
Ron Wheeler

ISBN 10 - 0615728375
ISBN 13 - 978-0615728377

All rights reserved
No part of this publication may be reproduced, stored in a retrieval system or transmitted in any form or by any means without the prior permission in writing of the publisher, nor be otherwise circulated in any form of binding or cover other than that in which it is published.

Acknowledgements

To the God of the Universe who gives and gives and gives even more: For all the times I believed you weren't there or didn't care, I'm sorry. For all the times you fiercely protected and gently carried me, I'm thankful. For all eternity that I will hear you call me by name, I'm amazed. I'm humbled by the reach of your love.

To Alexander Charles, Rachel Elizabeth, and Stephen Clay - my extravagant gifts from God: you hold the deepest places in my heart. I love you. God loves you so much more.

To Jill: For encouraging me to find God in the sandbox.

And to Richard: For being patient with me on the journey and for holding on to hope.

Dear Parent,

Having been raised in a Christian home with a strong working knowledge of the Bible, it was not until I was in my 30s that I began to realize my core beliefs – the reality that shapes who we are and how we view the rest of the world – were deeply flawed. I assumed that what I had always believed about God, myself, and my relationship with Him was true. However, there were parts and pieces missing, and my life was tragic evidence of a deeply wounded heart.

These chapters were born out of my desire to see children from a very early age begin to understand how incredibly valuable they are to God and how uniquely personal He is to each of us. In a day and age where society's culture is bombarding our children with the idea that nothing is sacred, values are no longer worth protecting, and the only goal worth pursuing is to gratify the flesh, I hear a desperate cry for someone to please tell these kids they are special - and why. I am convinced that boys want to believe they are not mere animals to conquer or be conquered and equally convinced that girls want to believe they have more to offer than an over-exposed shell of their true selves.

I hope *God's Pinky Promises* will offer your children an opportunity to fully embrace that they are of infinite value to their Creator. This is not a one-time read. Read these chapters together and discuss them often until the truths take root in your child's heart. Part of this was written for my own healing; a somewhat selfish attempt to re-capture pieces of what I lost as a child. The other part is simply to see my children and those around them grow up with the fundamental, rock solid conviction that they are loved by a God who is passionately pursuing relationship *with* them rather than checking off a 'to-do' list *for* them.

Billy Graham once said, "The word of God hidden in the heart of a child is a stubborn voice to suppress." My prayer is that these chapters will help you instill in your child a fascination with God and His Word to stubbornly protect for the rest of their lives.

Squeezing my heart out for Him,

For the children:

God loved the world so much that He gave us Jesus...

and then He gave us you.

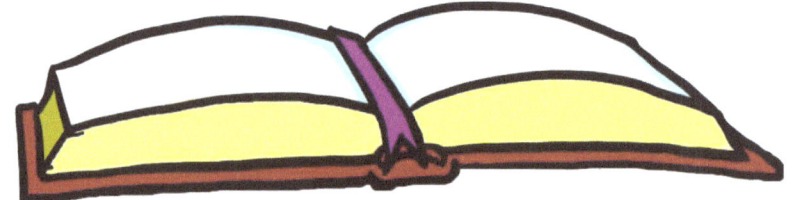

Hello, friend!

We are so excited that you are reading *God's Pinky Promises*. Our book is full of wonderful things for you to learn about God and how special you are to Him. We are going to be with you every step of the way, helping you learn to dig deep into God's Word and keep it safely in your heart.

We love to play in the dirt so come on, let's get started!
.

God's Pinky Promises

Chapter 1
God's Love ~ He IS Love!

Chapter 2
God's Creation ~ Seven Special Days

Chapter 3
God's Protection ~ The 10 Commandments

Chapter 4
God's Discipline ~ Why He Punishes Sin

Chapter 5
God's Forgiveness ~ Jesus

Chapter 6
God's Spirit ~ Hearing His Voice

Chapter 7
God's Passion ~ YOU!

Let's Explore...
God's Love ~ He IS Love!

Scratch the surface...

"Give thanks to the God of heaven! His love is eternal"
Psalms 136:26

Move the dirt around…

In the Hebrew language that God uses in the Old Testament, the word love is "Ahava", which means "I give". We learn from this that when God says He is love, it means He gives – of Himself and all He created. *Loving* is *giving*. And He gives us so much!

He gives us a family to help us feel secure
He gives us a place to live so we can be safe and warm
He gives us good food to eat so our bodies are healthy and strong
He gives us pets to play with and care for
He gives us rest so that our mind and body can be refreshed

He gives us the Bible, His very personal (and very long) letter to each of us
He gives us churches where we can share praise and worship together
He gives us Jesus, so we can live with Him forever in Heaven
He gives us the Holy Spirit, to help us know how to live for Him

He gives us all of creation to enjoy and explore
He gives us schools where we learn about the world around us
He gives us music and art to celebrate beauty in our world
He gives us friends to share our happy and sad times

You see, God's love is forever – God's giving of Himself to us is forever, too!

We'll look at more of the things God gives us in our other chapters. Can you think of some other things God has given you?

Uncover something new…

Doesn't it make you feel good inside when someone notices and says 'thank you' for something you've given them? It makes God happy when we say 'thank you' to Him, too. When we pray, God doesn't want us to try to use big words or say things we don't understand. He just wants us to talk to Him like we would talk to our best friend. It's that simple! Why don't you try it?

"Thank you, God, for your Ahava love.
Help me see the things you give me every day.
Please teach me to give love the way you do.
Amen."

Dig a little deeper...

With your parent's help, read the following verses and then see if you can answer the questions. You may even want to underline them in your own Bible.

Psalms 136:1 (hint: Old Testament)
"Give thanks to the Lord, for He is good. His love is eternal."

Question: How long does God's love last?

Ezekiel 36:26 (hint: Old Testament)
"I will give you a new heart and put a new spirit in you..."

Question: What does God promise to give you?

Romans 5:8 (hint: New Testament)
"But God proves His own love for us in that while we were still sinners Christ died for us!"

Question: What did God do for you?

Pack it in Memory Verse…

Find this verse in your Bible, highlight it, and memorize it ☺

I John 4:16
"And we have come to know and to believe the love that God has for us. God is love, and the one who remains in love remains in God, and God remains in him."

Let's Explore...

God's Creation ~ Seven Special Days

Scratch the surface...

"God saw all that He had made, and it was very good"
Genesis 1:30

Move the dirt around…

God knew even before time began that He would create the world as a beautiful place to put *us* – His most amazing creation of all!

God's order for things is always good and productive. He knew exactly what He was doing when He created the world and everything in it.

Day 1 – Light

The very first thing God created was Light. Do you think it was so He could see what He was doing? God separated the darkness from the light and called them 'night' and 'day'. That way, we know when to go to sleep and when to get up!

Day 2 – The Sky

God separated the earth from the sky. This is what we call our 'atmosphere' and it contains all the air we need to live and breathe. God separated the water on the earth from the clouds in the sky. The water on the earth evaporates and the clouds in the sky give us rain - a continuous perfect cycle.

Day 3 – Oceans, Dry Land, Plants and Trees

God separated the dry land from all the bodies of water in the world: oceans, seas, lakes, rivers, and creeks. Some are salty and some are not. Do you live near any bodies of water?

God also created plants and trees on this day, some that live on land and some that live under water. These are the plants and trees that give us seeds to grow and fruit to eat. They also give us oxygen to breathe. What is your favorite fruit?

Day 4 – The Sun, Moon, and Stars

God created the sun to warm the earth during the day, and the moon to give us light during the night. He created the stars so we can see them when it's dark. Do you think stars are God's 'night lights' for the angels?

Did you know that God calls every star by name? Just think how much more important you are than a star in the sky hundreds of millions of miles away!

Day 5 – Water creatures and Birds

God created the living things in all the bodies of water: whales, sharks, starfish, freshwater fish, crawdads, tadpoles, and little tiny 'amoebae' that we can't even see with our eyes! He also created all the beautiful birds that we see flying in the sky. Small little sparrows and huge eagles – God created them all.

Can you name your favorite fish? How about your favorite bird?

Day 6 – Land animals, Man and Woman

God created all the living things on land: bears, lizards, lions, horses, cows, puppies and kittens, and everything else that lives on the land. If you could be an animal, what would you be? Why?

After all this, God created His greatest masterpiece of all – Adam and Eve. God created Adam out of the dirt on the ground! Do you think that's why kids like to play in the dirt? After God created Adam, He created Eve from one of Adam's ribs. Don't worry though, God put Adam in a deep sleep so he didn't feel a thing.

Day 7 – God rested

God didn't need to rest because He was tired (the Bible teaches us that God never sleeps, snoozes, or takes a nap!). He rested because He was finished and everything was perfect. Ahhhhh…

Uncover something new

God rested from the work of creation so He could enjoy it. He probably wanted to spend some time with Adam and Eve, too. Doesn't it feel good to rest for a little while when you've finished your work? Go ahead -- enjoy spending time with your friends and family.

"Thank you, God, for all of your creation – especially me!
Help me to show respect for everything in your world.
Please teach me to love others as you do.
Amen."

Dig a little deeper...

With your parent's help, read the following verses and then see if you can answer the questions. You may even want to find them in your own Bible.

(Hint: all these verses are in the very first book of the Bible, Genesis)

Genesis 1:1
"In the beginning God created the heavens and the earth."

Question: When did God create heaven and earth?

Genesis 1:3
"Then God said, 'Let there be light,' and there was light."

Question: What happened after God said, 'let there be light'?

Genesis 2:3
God blessed the seventh day and declared it holy, and He rested from His work of creation."

Question: What did God say about the seventh day?

Pack it in Memory Verse...

Find this verse in your Bible, highlight it and memorize it ☺

Genesis 1:27
"So God created people in His own image; He created people in the image of God; He created them male and female."

Let's Explore...

God's Protection ~ The 10 Commandments

Scratch the surface…

"Make Your ways known to me, Lord; teach me your paths"
Psalms 25:4

Move the dirt around...

God gave us the Ten Commandments because He loves us (remember Ahava love?) and He knows the consequences of stepping outside that love.

"Consequences" is a big word that means 'results'. If we pour too much milk in a glass, it will spill out. The milk that spills is the consequence of pouring too much in the glass. Got it?

When your parents teach you not to walk in the street or put your hand on a hot stove, do you think they are trying to protect you or punish you? Of course, they're trying to protect you and keep you from getting hurt!

This is the same reason God gives us the Ten Commandments – He wants to protect our heart from getting hurt and guide us into a wonderful life. Let's take a look at these very special instructions God gave to us.

1.
"You should have no other gods before me"
Nothing deserves our praise and worship except God. We are His most valuable creation and He is the only one who should have first place in our heart.

2.
"Do not make an idol for yourself"
An idol is anything (or anyone) that becomes more important in our life than God.

3.
"Use the name of God carefully"
God's name is special and holy. We should always give Him honor when we say it.

4.
"Make Sunday a special day every week"
Sunday is a day to join with others at church to worship God, learn from our Sunday School teachers and pastor, enjoy God's creation, and relax with our family.

5.
"Show respect to your parents"
God made no mistake when He placed you in your family. Even when we don't like the rules we are given, God will bless us for being respectful and obedient.

6.
"Don't kill another person out of anger"
Sometimes people do or say things that make us angry. But they are still God's creation, even when they behave in an unkind way. It's ok to feel angry. Just remember that God loves both of you.

7.
"Love your husband or wife in a special way"

God created marriage when He created Adam and Eve. Marriage is a special promise that two people make only to each other. The Bible teaches us that God's desire is for us to always be faithful and true to that promise.

8.
"Don't take what doesn't belong to you"

When we take things that are not ours - even if no one else finds out - our heart knows. God knows that guilt will make us want to hide and He doesn't ever want us to be separated from Him!

9.
"Don't tell a lie"

It hurts when people say things that aren't true. God created us in His image, to be like Him. When we tell a lie, we are not telling the truth about God in us. Ouch!

10.
"Be content with what is yours"

Wanting what someone else has keeps our mind on others instead of God. So be happy for what your friends have and be happy with what you have. And always be ready to share.

The first 4 commandments teach us about our relationship with God. The next 3 commandments teach us about our relationship with others, and the last 3 commandments teach us about our relationship with ourselves - our hands, our mouth, and our heart.

Uncover something new…

God's 10 Commandments are like fences to keep us happy and safe from things that pull our heart away from Him. Fences help us keep the good stuff in and the bad stuff out!

"Thank you, God, for the Ten Commandments.
Help me to stay inside your fences.
Please teach me to follow your instructions.
Amen."

Dig a little deeper...

With your parent's help, read the following verses and then see if you can answer the questions. You may even want to find them in your own Bible.

Joshua 1:7 (hint: Old Testament)
"Above all, be strong and very courageous to carefully observe the whole instruction my servant Moses commanded you...so that you will have success wherever you go."

Question: What are you to do with God's 'book of instruction'?

Psalms 32:8 (hint: Old Testament)
"I will instruct you and show you the way to go; with my eye on you, I will give you counsel."

Question: Who gives you guidance and direction?

Proverbs 8:33-35 (hint: Old Testament)
"Listen to instruction and be wise; don't' ignore it."

Question: Why should you listen to God's instruction?

Pack it in Memory Verse…

Find this verse in your Bible, highlight it and memorize it ☺

I Timothy 1:5 (hint: New Testament)
"Now the goal of our instruction is love from a pure heart, a good conscience, and a sincere faith."

Let's Explore...

God's Discipline ~ Why He Punishes Sin

Scratch the surface...

"The Lord disciplines those He loves, just as a parent disciplines their own child"
Proverbs 3:12

Move the dirt around...

God is perfect and holy – He never has and never will sin. When we sin, it builds a wall between our heart and God's.

God hates sin because He hates what it does to us. He never wants us to be separated from Him. He loves us. So He disciplines us to teach us.

It breaks God's heart for us to make wrong choices. Because He loves us, He gives us discipline to teach us right from wrong and help push sin out of our hearts.

Remember Ahava love? God is always giving His love, even when it means discipline. It is one of the kindest, most loving things God does - kind of like when our parents discipline us for running out into the street. They discipline us to protect us.

Even though discipline is painful, it teaches us that wrong choices get us in trouble.

Discipline makes us think about those wrong choices and God's desire is that we always think before we act.

God told Adam and Eve to stay away from the fruit of one tree in the Garden of Eden. In this huge, beautiful garden, God told them to stay away from just one tree! But they disobeyed, and God knew their hearts would be tempted to disobey again.

God still loved them but He also disciplined them because of their sin. Adam and Eve had to leave the Garden that God had created just for them; that was the consequence. His heart was broken because He was now separated from His most valuable creation. Their hearts were broken, too.

Just like Adam and Eve, God knows we are tempted every day to disobey. Discipline is one of the ways God teaches us to be careful about the choices we make. He wants us to remember what the Bible says before we make a choice that will hurt us.

Uncover something new...

The most important thing to learn about discipline is that even when we make wrong choices, God still loves us! He is unhappy with our sin, but He never ever stops loving us – not even for a second! That's what makes forgiveness so wonderful. We'll read more about Forgiveness in Chapter 5.

"Thank you, God, for punishment, even though it hurts.
Help me to not build a wall of sin between my heart and Yours.
Please teach me to make good choices.
Amen."

Dig a little deeper...

With your parent's help, read the following verses and then see if you can answer the questions. You may even want to find them in your own Bible.

Job 5:17 (hint: Old Testament)
"See how happy is the man God corrects; so do not reject the discipline of the Almighty."

Question: How should you respond to God's discipline?

Psalms 94:12 (hint: Old Testament)
"Lord, happy is the man you discipline and teach from your law."

Question: Where does discipline come from?

Hebrews 12:10 (hint: New Testament)
"...but God disciplines us for our benefit, so that we can share His holiness."

Question: Why does God discipline you?

Pack it in Memory Verse…

Find this verse in your Bible, highlight it and memorize it ☺

Proverbs 10:17 (hint: Old Testament)
"Whoever pays attention to discipline shows the way to life, but whoever ignores correction leads others astray."

Let's Explore...

God's Forgiveness ~ Jesus

Scratch the surface...

"God proves His love for us because while we were still sinners,
He sent Jesus Christ to die for us"
Romans 5:8

Move the dirt around…

God hates to be separated from us because of sin. His favorite thing in the whole world is to forgive us! And once He forgives us He chooses not to remember it anymore. He forgets … forever!

God knew when He created the world that there could only be one way to have forgiveness for our sin. That was the only way it could be offered to everyone.

Can you imagine how confusing it would be to have a different set of rules for different people all over the world? God's holiness required one perfect way of forgiveness and He lovingly gave us that perfect way in Jesus.

Jesus is God's Son, born to a young woman named Mary a long time ago in Bethlehem. God's perfect plan for Mary was to be the mother of Jesus. God has a perfect plan for you, too. We'll learn more about that in Chapter 7.

God's plan for Jesus was to become a human being just like us, so we could know that God is real and His forgiveness is real, too. This is God's plan of salvation for the whole world. Jesus was able to show us God's love, teach us how to obey, and help us learn to love each other.

Because Jesus lived a perfect life without ever disobeying or making a wrong choice, He was the only one who could die in our place – to take the punishment for our sin.

Imagine if a friend did something wrong and you decided to take the punishment that should have gone to your friend. It's like that, except that the sin of the whole world - yours and mine included - meant that Jesus had to *die* for God to be able to forgive us.

Jesus obeyed God's instructions for Him, even to the point of death! Aren't you glad that God will forgive us because of what Jesus did? God promises to forgive us every time we ask, every day of our lives, even if it's 100 times in a single day! The most important part for us is to admit that we've done wrong and ask for forgiveness.

When Jesus died on the cross it didn't mean that we would never sin again. It means that when we sin we are always able to ask for forgiveness. Do you ever feel that your sin keeps God from loving you? It's important to know what God says about forgiveness so we can tell ourselves the truth!

After Jesus died on the cross, He was in a grave for three days. And then God - because His Ahava love is always giving - brought Jesus back from the dead to live again! Jesus conquered death and sin so that we have everything we need: eternal life *and* forgiveness.

Uncover something new…

Jesus now lives in Heaven with God, waiting for the day when we will come live with Him, too. And from that day on, we won't ever have to worry about being tempted by sin ever again.

"Thank you, God, for giving us Jesus.
Help me give my life to Him.
Please teach me to love and follow Him always.
Amen."

Dig a little deeper...

With your parent's help, read the following verses and then see if you can answer the questions. You may even want to find them in your own Bible.

Psalms 103:12 (hint: Old Testament)
'As far as the east is from the west, so far has He removed our disobedience from us."

Question: How far does God's forgiveness go?

John 3:16 (hint: New Testament)
"For God so loved the world that He gave us His only son, that whoever believes in Him will not perish, but will have everlasting life."

Question: Why did God give you Jesus?

Acts 13:38 (hint: New Testament)
"...I want you to know that through Jesus, the forgiveness of sins has been made known to you."

Question: Who does forgiveness come through?

Pack it in Memory Verse...

Find this verse in your Bible, highlight it and memorize it ☺

Acts 10:43 (hint: New Testament)
"All the prophets testify about Him that through His name everyone who believes in Him will receive forgiveness of sins."

Let's Explore...

God's Spirit ~ Hearing His Voice

Scratch the surface...

"Teach me to do your will, for you are my God;
may your good Spirit lead me on level ground."
Psalms 143:10

Move the dirt around...

Thank goodness God doesn't just give us the 10 Commandments we studied in Chapter 3 and then leave us on our own! He gave us Jesus but then He gave us even more! Before Jesus went to Heaven, He promised to send someone very special, someone who would help us remember in our heart everything God wants us to know.

Think about a time when Mom or Dad said not to have any more snacks before dinner. But you were SO hungry and you took a snack anyway. Remember that little voice inside your head that told you not to do it?

Or how about when someone asked you how a toy got broken and you told a lie? Remember that little voice inside your head that told you it was wrong?

God gives us that very special voice – it's called a 'conscience'. Our conscience helps us remember the difference between right and wrong. When we are asking God to help us obey, He gives us the Holy Spirit to guide our conscience and help us hear Him loud and clear.

When we pray, we can ask God for anything and tell Him everything. He's never too busy to listen! But after we have talked to God, we need to get quiet and listen – in our heart – and allow God to talk to us through the Holy Spirit.

Sometimes it's easy to hear what the Holy Spirit is saying, sometimes it's hard. It might be an easy thing like thanking your family for taking good care of you. Or it might be something exciting like using part of your allowance for a special project at church or in your community. It might be something hard like forgiving someone who has hurt you. It might even be asking someone to forgive you for hurting them.

God promises to always guide us when we ask Him for direction. He does that through the voice of the Holy Spirit in our heart. And He promises us that His way is easiest. Even when it seems hard, it's always for our good. Why? Because God's Ahava love is always giving and God always gives what is best.

The Bible teaches us that the Holy Spirit's voice is soft and quiet. God is a gentleman and He won't yell at us to get our attention. He wants us to be still and quiet so we can hear Him clearly. And if we accidentally fall asleep while we're listening, it's ok! We've just taken a nap in the strong, loving arms of our Heavenly Father!

Uncover something new...

Prayer is one of the best ways to learn to hear God's voice. Reading the Bible is another way to learn to hear His voice, too. You might also draw pictures to remind you what you've talked to God about. The Holy Spirit is alive in our hearts – we can ask Him anything, anytime, anywhere!

"Thank you, God, for giving us the Holy Spirit.
Help me be still and quiet so I can hear.
Teach me to listen with my heart and follow where you lead.
Amen."

Dig a little deeper…

With your parent's help, read the following verses and then see if you can answer the questions. You may even want to find them in your own Bible.

Jeremiah 24:7 (hint: Old Testament)
"I will give them a heart to know me, that I am the LORD. They will be my people, and I will be their God, for they will return to me with all their heart."

Question: Where does hearing God's voice begin?

John 14:26 (hint: New Testament)
But the Counselor, the Holy Spirit … will teach you all things and remind you of everything I have told you."

Question: What is another name for the Holy Spirit?

2nd Timothy 1:14 (hint: New Testament)
"Guard, through the Holy Spirit who lives in us, that good thing entrusted to you."

Question: Who helps you obey God?

Pack it in Memory Verse...

Find this verse in your Bible, highlight it and memorize it ☺

Luke 11:28 (hint: New Testament)
"Blessed are those who hear the word of God and obey it."

Let's Explore...

God's Passion ~ YOU!

Scratch the surface...

"I will praise you, because I have been remarkably and wonderfully made"
Psalms 139:14

Move the dirt around...

Did you know that before God created the world, He had you in His heart and mind? He knew the exact day and time you would be born and all of Heaven rejoiced when you took your first breath.

God knew what color your hair and eyes would be, and He knew what your parents would name you. God's Word says that before you were born, He had already counted the hairs on your head and written out every day of your life!

He knew if you would have freckles, be short or tall, where you would live, and what your favorite foods would be.

God also knew what would hurt and disappoint you. He knew every time you would shed a tear – He has a bottle in heaven with your name on it and He keeps your tears there!

Nothing about your life is a surprise to God. That's because He is absolutely, totally, completely and unconditionally fascinated with YOU!

There is nothing you can ever do or say to make Him stop loving you. Even when you disobey, He still loves you and longs for your heart to be right with His.

When we go through things that are hard or sad God has not forgotten us, not even for a moment. Not one single thing in our life ever happens without Him knowing about it first.

He knows us better than anyone and there's no safer place for us to be than under His protection because everything He does is for our good.

Uncover something new…

God's ahava love gives us Jesus so that we have forgiveness. He gives us the Holy Spirit to help us hear His voice. And He gives each of us a special purpose in life that no one else can fulfill. Everything God does is because of us, for us, and about us. Wow! I feel special, don't you?

"Thank you, God, for creating me just the way I am.
Help me remember that you are crazy about me!
Please teach me to understand how special I am to you.
Amen."

Dig a little deeper...

With your parent's help, read the following verses and then see if you can answer the questions. You may even want to find them in your own Bible.

Psalms 139:2-4
"You know when I sit and when I stand; you understand my thoughts from far away.
You know when I am playing and when I am still; you know all my ways.
Before a word is in my mouth you know it completely, Lord."

Question: What does God know about you?

Psalms 139:13
"For you created my inmost being; you knit me together in my mother's womb."

Question: How did God put you together?

Jeremiah 29:11
"For I know the plans I have for you, says the Lord, plans for good and not evil,
to give you a future and a hope."

Question: Does God have a plan for you?

Pack it in Memory Verse…

Find this verse in your Bible, highlight it and memorize it ☺

Zephaniah 3:17
"The LORD your God is with you, he is mighty to save. He will take great delight in you, he will quiet you with his love, he will rejoice over you with singing."

Let's Review God's Pinky Promises...

In Chapter 1, we learned about God's "Ahava" love: Loving is giving and God gives us a world full of wonderful things!

In Chapter 2, we learned about God's creation: Seven special days and one super-special day when YOU were created!

In Chapter 3, we learned about God's protection: He gave us the 10 Commandments, which help to protect our hearts.

In Chapter 4, we learned about God's discipline: Punishment for sin is God's way of teaching us to think about what we do before we do it.

In Chapter 5, we learned about God's forgiveness: Jesus is God's incredible gift, showing us that His forgiveness is real.

In Chapter 6, we learned about God's Spirit: God loves it when we get quiet and listen to what His voice, His Spirit, is saying to us.

In Chapter 7, we learned about God's passion: YOU are His most amazing creation and He is head over heels in love with you!

More from this Author:

A guide for growing a marriage of joy and satisfaction as it was intended by The Master Gardener.

Told in touching photographs and the wisdom of many voices, it is a treasure of insight for couples just starting out in married life, and those who have spent decades joyfully tending their garden.

Available at Amazon and other fine booksellers.

About the Author:

Dawn Hood is many things: a Southerner, a mother of three, a cancer survivor, a Georgia Bulldogs fan, a lover of ice cream, Christmas music, and words. Her experiences are her pen, her heart her inkwell. As she said when she delivered her first manuscript, "You now have my soul on paper."

We hope you've enjoyed exploring God's love and His special message for you. If you have more questions, talk to your parents, your grandparents, your minister or Sunday School teacher.
Parents, if you have questions, comments or constructive criticism, you can reach Dawn Hood at:
DawnCH@inknbeans.com

To know more about Dawn, visit her website at:
AuthorDawnHood.com

Many thanks to Ron Wheeler for capturing the author's vision of Bucky and Scoop and bringing a spirit of joy and discovery to this journey.

www.ingramcontent.com/pod-product-compliance
Lightning Source LLC
LaVergne TN
LVHW072112070426
835510LV00002B/24